From Me to You

Written by Joshua Hatch
Series Consultant: Linda Hoyt

Contents

Introduction

Whenever you hear a baby cry, believe it or not, the crying baby is trying to get a message across. Maybe the baby has a wet nappy, or is tired or hungry. Crying is one of the ways that babies communicate what they need, but it doesn't tell you exactly what the problem is.

Luckily, babies grow and develop into toddlers and learn words. Then they can say, "I'm hungry!" Using words is a much better way of communicating because you can be specific about what you want to say.

Try this

Think of some body language or facial expressions that communicate specific thoughts or feelings. Show them to some friends and see if they can guess what you're trying to communicate.

Words are just one way to communicate. We also use body language, facial expressions and tone of voice.

Technology also affects how people communicate. Many thousands of years ago, people didn't have pens and paper, or mobile phones, or the Internet for communication. Today we do.

This book explores how people communicate and the role technology plays in communications.

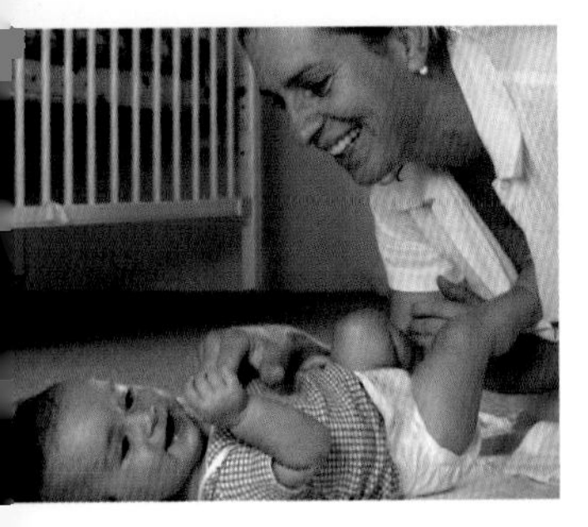

Chapter 1

Ways of communicating

Face-to-face communication

People use language and body movements to communicate with people near them.

Learning to talk

From birth, babies are surrounded by people who talk not only to them, but also to each other. Human babies seem to have an inbuilt ability to recognise speech sounds and link them with objects. They begin to "speak" by making sounds. Gradually, children start using words and then begin to put those words together in phrases and sentences.

Children learn language by listening to others.

Languages people speak

There are almost 7,000 spoken languages now used by people throughout the world. Some languages, such as English and Spanish, are used widely by many people around the world. Other languages are spoken only by a few people who live in the same area and are not used elsewhere.

Making gestures
Facial expressions and body gestures are ways to communicate.

Facial expressions are the ways people change their faces to show emotion. Body gestures are the way people stand or sit or move their hands and feet.

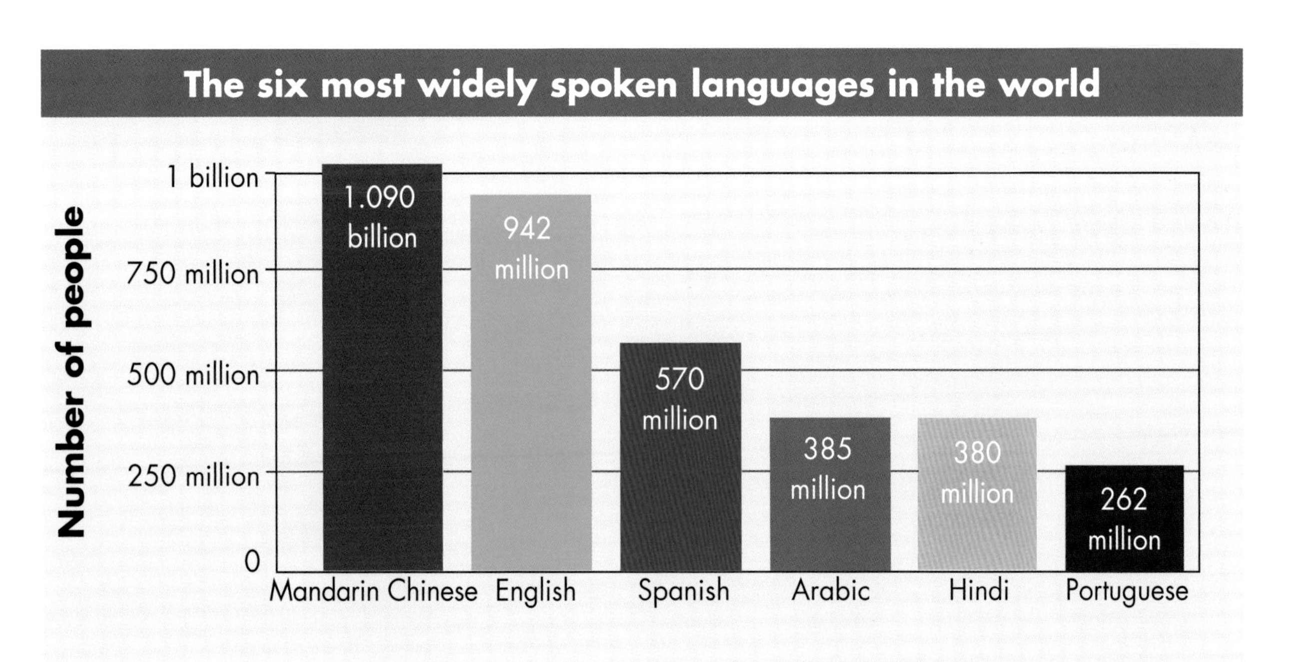

The written word

Written messages made it possible for people to communicate over distance and over time.

Words in pictures

Thousands of years ago, people began to draw pictures of animals, people and the world around them. Sometimes when the pictures were put together they told a story. Some of these drawings were made on cave walls and still exist today.

Ancient Egyptians recorded their lives and told stories using pictures and symbols, which were called **hieroglyphics**. They carved hieroglyphics into stones. Today, these hieroglyphics help us understand what life was like for the ancient Egyptians.

There are some languages, such as Mandarin Chinese, that use only symbols for words.

Some examples of Mandarin Chinese symbols and their English translation

Alphabets

The English language uses letters to create words. By combining just a few letters in different ways, many words can be created. The 26 letters in English can spell about 500,000 words.

The alphabet used in English is just one of many alphabets. It is known as the Latin or Roman alphabet because it came from ancient Roman times. English, German, Italian, French and Spanish are all based on the same alphabet.

Cyrillic alphabet

In Russia, the Cyrillic alphabet is used to write words. There are 33 letters in this alphabet and some do not have a corresponding English letter.

Some Russian letters look strange to English readers, while others look familiar. And some that look the same, sound different. In Russian, "B" sounds like an English "V".

А	К	Х
Б	Л	Ц
В	М	Ч
Г	Н	Ш
Д	О	Щ
Е	П	ъ
Ё	Р	ы
Ж	С	ь
З	Т	Э
И	У	Ю
Й	Ф	Я

Try this

Passing on a spoken message isn't always as accurate as sending a written message. See for yourself. Sit in a circle with friends. Whisper something to the person on your left. Have them whisper the same thing to the person on their left. Keep going around the circle. When you get the message back, is it the same as what you first said?

Ways of writing

Once people developed ways to write, they could communicate over distance. No longer did people have to be in the same place at the same time in order to communicate. One person could write down a message and send it to someone else, or the message could be saved to be read later.

Today, we can read the writings from long ago and find out what people thought about and how they lived.

Chapter 2

Making connections

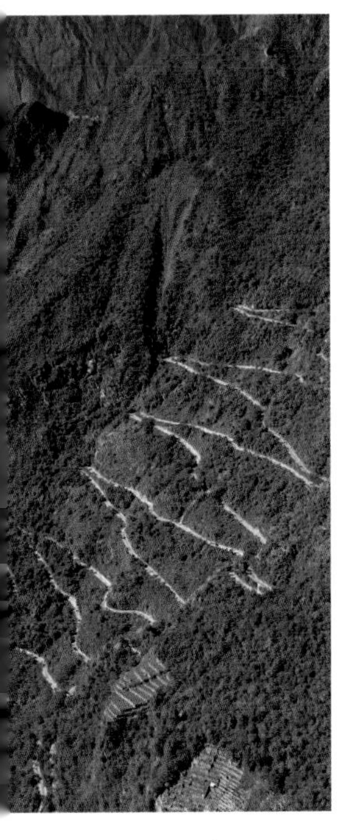

Zigzag paths built during the Incan Empire

People invented new ways for messages to be communicated quickly over long distances.

Many centuries ago, the Incan people in South America travelled on foot to relay messages to each other. The roads they used weren't like modern roads. They were more like well-worn paths. The **messengers** were so fast that a message could travel hundreds of kilometres in a single day.

Once electrical communication was developed, information was able to be transmitted over long distances. The telegraph was a machine that sent electrical signals that were received almost immediately over a wire.

The Pony Express
Before the telegraph system opened in the United States, mail was sent across the country using the Pony Express. It took about 10 days to cover nearly 3,000 kilometres.

Samuel Morse

A leap of imagination

Samuel Morse invented his own telegraph system – Morse code.

In Morse code, every letter and number has a pattern of dots and dashes. The telegrapher would tap the key for a dot or hold down the key for a dash. When the dots and dashes were received, they were turned into letters so the message could be read.

Morse code began to be used in the United States in 1844. From then the telegraph spread quickly to many countries around the world.

Morse code						**Numbers**	
A	•–	J	•–––	S	•••	0	–––––
B	–•••	K	–•–	T	–	1	•––––
C	–•–•	L	•–••	U	••–	2	••–––
D	–••	M	––	V	•••–	3	•••––
E	•	N	–•	W	•––	4	••••–
F	••–•	O	–––	X	–••–	5	•••••
G	––•	P	•––•	Y	–•––	6	–••••
H	••••	Q	––•–	Z	––••	7	––•••
I	••	R	•–•			8	–––••
						9	––––•

Sending telegrams

Messages sent by Morse code came to be known as telegrams. People could now communicate with each other nearly instantly, as long as a cable connected them.

Messages were sent to the local telegraph office, turned into letters and words, printed out and then delivered by hand. It took two to three days for a telegram to be delivered.

Post Office Telegraph Headquarters, London, England, 1871

Try this

Cracking the code

Can you decode this Morse-coded message?

−.−− −−− ..−

−.. .. −..

.. − !

(Find the answer on page 23)

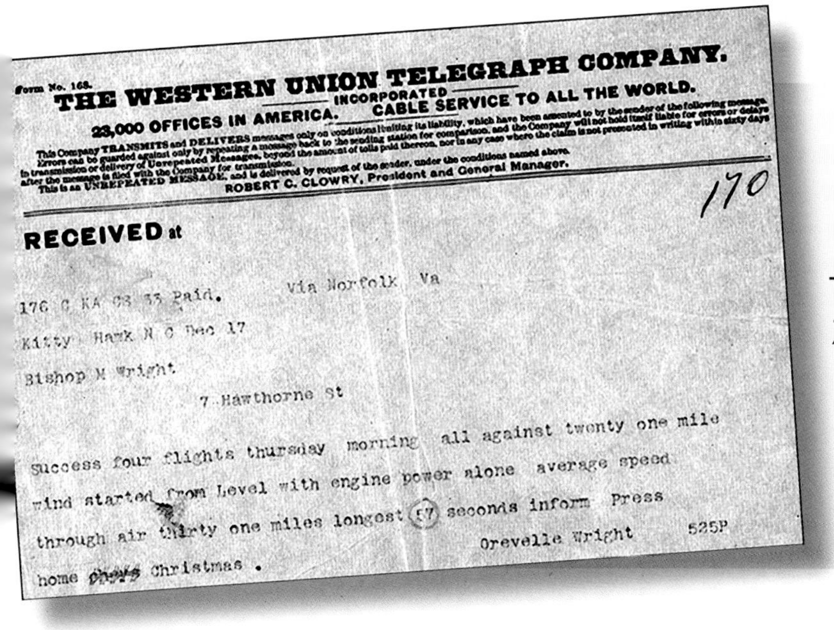

Form No. 168.

THE WESTERN UNION TELEGRAPH COMPANY.

INCORPORATED

23,000 OFFICES IN AMERICA. CABLE SERVICE TO ALL THE WORLD.

This Company TRANSMITS and DELIVERS messages only on conditions limiting its liability, which have been assented to by the sender of the following message. Errors can be guarded against only by repeating a message back to the sending station for comparison, and the Company will not hold itself liable for errors or delays in transmission or delivery of Unrepeated Messages, beyond the amount of tolls paid thereon, nor in any case where the claim is not presented in writing within sixty days after the message is filed with the Company for transmission.

This is an UNREPEATED MESSAGE, and is delivered by request of the sender, under the conditions named above.

ROBERT C. CLOWRY, President and General Manager.

170

RECEIVED at

176 C KA CS 33 Paid. Via Norfolk Va

Kitty Hawk N C Dec 17

Bishop M Wright

7 Hawthorne St

Success four flights thursday morning all against twenty one mile wind started from Level with engine power alone average speed through air thirty one miles longest 57 seconds inform Press home Christmas .

Orevelle Wright 525P

Did you know?

The first Australia to New Zealand telegraph was received in 1876.

Find out more
What did Alexander Graham Bell say when he transmitted the first words by telephone?

The telephone and beyond

Alexander Graham Bell invented the telephone in 1876. Now, speech could be transmitted electronically. By the end of 1880, there were 47,900 telephones in the United States.

The telephone was so popular that telephone companies had to string **overhead** wires everywhere so that people could be connected to the telephone. In more than 140 years, the telephone has changed society and society has changed the telephone.

A 1920s telephone

A recent telephone

A 1960s dial telephone

Mobile telephones

Originally all telephones had to be connected to a telephone line, and could be used only at a fixed point. But mobile phones work differently. Mobile phones communicate through **radio waves**. Your mobile phone sends a radio wave out. It goes in all directions until it hits a phone tower. The tower will then send a radio wave to the phone of the person you want to talk to.

Basic mobile phones have limited functions. They can make and receive calls, send text messages and even email. Advanced mobile phones, called smart phones, can do much more. They connect to the Internet, record and send photos and videos, play games, run apps and much more. They are powerful computers that are always online.

Did you know?

More than 88 per cent of people in Australia have a mobile phone.

Mobile phones are the most popular electronic gadgets in history. It is estimated that there are more mobile phones than people in the world — more than 7 billion.

Chapter 3

Riding the Internet wave

Computers were first built in the 1940s, but they were unable to communicate with one another. Over time, new technologies like **modems** were invented. They allowed computers to be connected across a network. The most famous network is the Internet.

Computers send **data** to each other over a telephone line. The data can be text, audio or video. Now, people on opposite sides of the world can have real-time video chats with each other.

Communicating online

Email

Back when it could take days, weeks or months to deliver a letter, people wrote long and detailed letters and the sender wouldn't expect a reply for weeks or maybe even years. With the development of email, we can write short notes, ask quick questions and reply with brief answers. We can also send the same email to a group of people. Now people expect instant answers and many people get more email than they can manage.

Thanks to email, things that were impossible before are now simple. People who live in different parts of the world can work together using email and the Internet.

Spam

Email security, however, is a growing problem. **Scammers** are people who send emails trying to get people's bank account numbers, passwords or other private information. These emails are one type of spam, a term used for any unwanted junk mail received over the Internet.

Spam can also include advertisements and offers to sell things. You should not reply to spam emails, because it increases the likelihood of more spam being sent.

Did you know?

It is estimated that 60 per cent of email sent on the Internet is spam.

Real-time conversations

Today, people use text, audio and video to have real-time conversations.

Using phone texting or chat programs, people can write short Instant Messages (IMs) to each other, or to groups of people at once. Text messages are often short, so people developed abbreviations like LOL for "laugh out loud". They also created emoticons, which were shortcuts for emotions. Typing a colon, hyphen and close parenthesis made a happy face :-).

More recently, hundreds of little pictures, called emoji, have been created, allowing you to write messages like this:

Mum:   ?

Me: 

Social media

People use social media to share their thoughts, photos and videos with each other. Hundreds or thousands of people can quickly see one person's post.

Social media is a powerful way to connect people, but it is not always safe. Some people aren't who they say they are online. Also, some people think they are anonymous online, but that's not always the case. It's easy to share personal information without realising it.

Cyberbullying

Bullying happens when a person teases or bothers another person. Bullying can happen on the Internet too – it's called cyberbullying. If children or teenagers are contacted by cyberbullies they should not respond. Instead they should tell an adult about it.

Tips for staying safe online

1. Keep your passwords private.
2. Send only the types of messages you would like to receive, and that you are sure will not hurt others.
3. If you feel bullied or anyone makes you uncomfortable online, do not respond. Tell a teacher or parent.
4. Keep personal information private. Don't give out information such as your second name, password, phone number, address, school, clubs you belong to or other activities you do.
5. No network is completely secure. If you see something that is confusing or makes you feel uncomfortable, tell a teacher or your parents.

The Internet: The good and the bad

The Internet is like anything else – you can use it for good or for bad purposes. Two debating teams are preparing to debate the pros and cons of the Internet.

The team FOR

Speaker one

Our team will need to convince everyone of the benefits of the Internet. I will explore how the Internet provides faster communication, and how distance does not affect how long it takes for people to communicate with each other.

Speaker two

I will research how using the Internet means that conversations don't have to happen in real time. If you want to talk to someone who's not available, you can send an email. Using email, people can respond when they have time. Email conversations can be very short or they can last days or weeks.

Speaker three

I will argue that the Internet makes it easy to get a wide range of information. On the Internet you can find hundreds of Web pages filled with useful information. Never has information been as widely available.

The team AGAINST

Speaker one

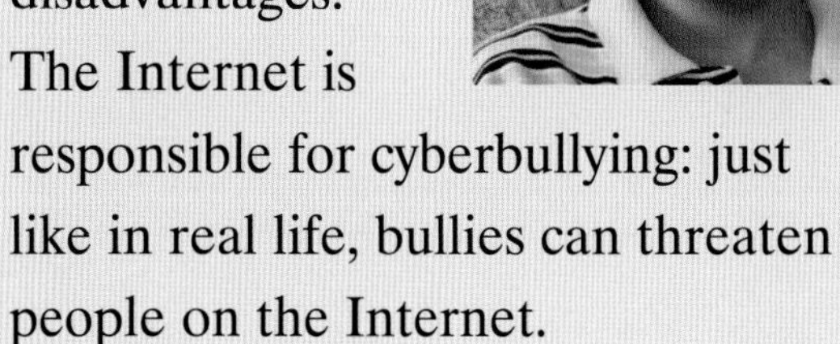

Our team is going to show that the Internet has many disadvantages. The Internet is responsible for cyberbullying: just like in real life, bullies can threaten people on the Internet.

Speaker two

I'm going to investigate how much spam people get and the types of spam there are. Spam can fill your email in-box and keep real email from getting through. What is worse, some spam carry attachments with a **virus** that can harm your computer.

Speaker three

I will look into how some people become addicted to the Internet. This can happen when you download a game and can't stop playing it. This is not good for you because it is harmful to your brain.

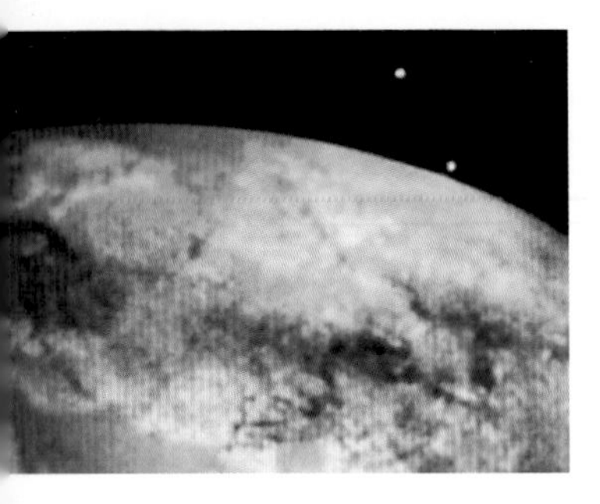

Conclusion

The technology that enables us to communicate in different ways has developed rapidly – not just in the past **century** but also in the past **decade.** So, what's next?

Computers are getting better at recognising our voices, allowing us to dictate letters or to give simple instructions. Imagine if you didn't have to speak at all. What if you could just think? Scientists are working on helmets that monitor brain activity and convert thoughts to control a computer.

But for now, if you want to communicate with someone, you will just have to use one of the methods that already exist!

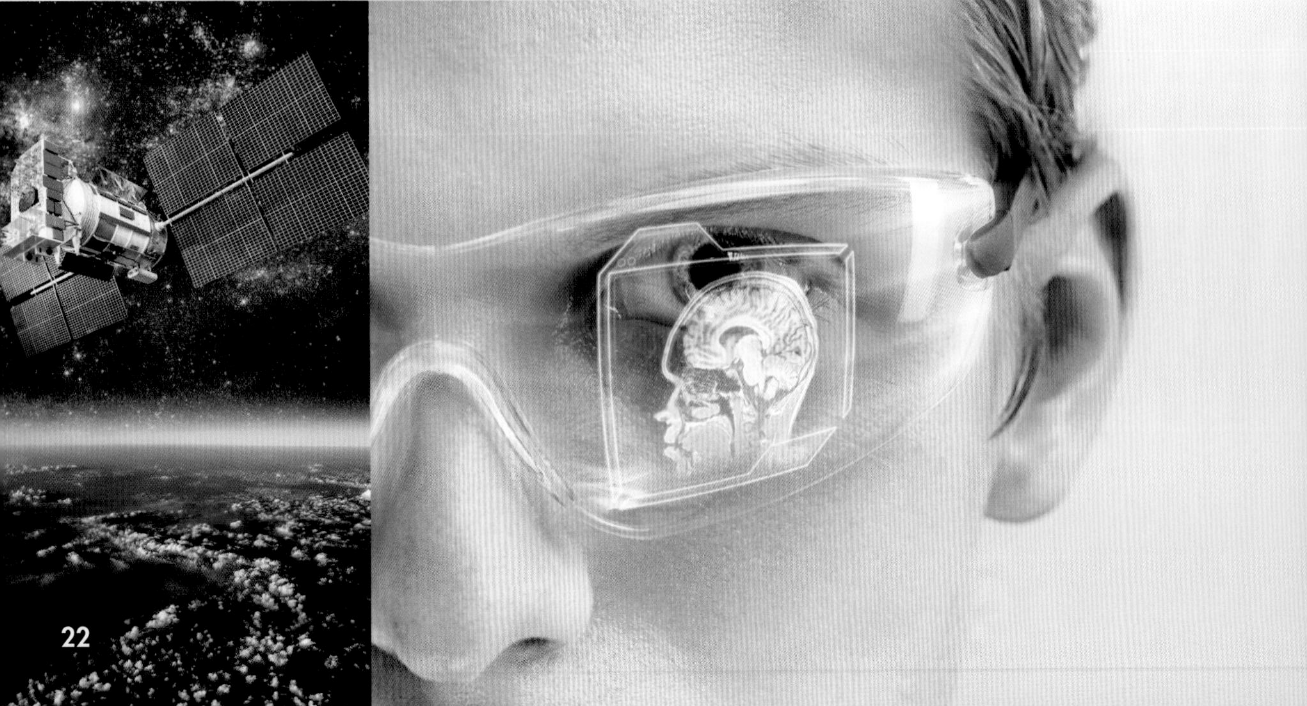

Glossary

century 100 years

continents large land masses, often made up of several countries

data a collection of information

decade 10 years

hieroglyphics the way of writing symbols used mainly by ancient Egyptians

messengers people who deliver messages

modems device that allows computers to share information

overhead when something is above the ground, especially high enough to be over people's heads

radio waves signals that are sent without wires

scammers people who attempt to obtain money by deceiving others

sequence the order in which one thing follows after another

virus a code added to a program that can seriously damage a computer when opened

(Page 13, Cracking the code, answer: You did it!)

Index